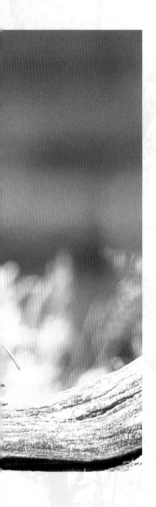

CONTENTS

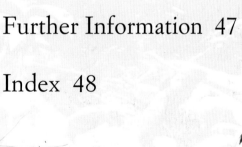

THE RAINFOREST HOME

Tropical rainforests are home to some of the world's most unusual and secretive mammals. Tropical regions are found near the Equator, between the tropics of Cancer and Capricorn. They are areas where temperatures are high and rainfall is greater than 2,000 mm every year. Tropical rainforests are found in parts of South and Central America, Africa, South-east Asia and Australasia.

The Amazon region of South America is the largest area of continuous rainforest on earth. In the Amazon rainforest, jaguars prowl the twilight world of the forest floor in search of deer and wild pigs, called peccaries. Tapirs and capybaras move quietly across the forest floor, plunging into

◀ (Above left) Big cats roam the floor of a variety of forest types including the rainforests of Asia. The tiger is the largest member of the cat family. Today, there are fewer thàn 6,000 tigers left in the wild.

▲ (Above right) Rainforests are home to a wide variety of mammals that live in trees. Many species of monkey, such as this titi monkey from the Amazon rainforest, swing through the branches of the rainforest canopy.

RAINFOREST
MAMMALS

Text and photography by Edward Parker

an imprint of Hodder Children's Books

© 2002 White-Thomson Publishing Ltd

Produced for Hodder Wayland by
White-Thomson Publishing Ltd
2/3 St. Andrew's Place
Lewes, East Sussex
BN7 1UP

Editor: Sarah Doughty
Design: Bernard Higton
Text consultant: Dr Paul Toyne

Published in Great Britain in 2002 by Hodder Wayland,
an imprint of Hodder Children's Books.
This paperback edition published in 2003

The right of Edward Parker to be identified as the author
and photographer has been asserted by him in accordance
with the Copyright, Designs and Patents Act 1988.

Produced in association with WWF-UK.
WWF-UK registered charity number 1081247.
A company limited by guarantee number 4016725. Panda
device © 1986 WWF ® WWF registered trademark
owner.

British Library Cataloguing in Publication Data
   Parker, Edward
   Mammals. – (Rainforests)
   Rainforest animals   2. Mammals
   I. Title   599.1'734
ISBN 0 7502 3813 5

Printed in Hong Kong

Hodder Children's Books
A division of Hodder Headline Limited
338 Euston Road, London NW1 3BH

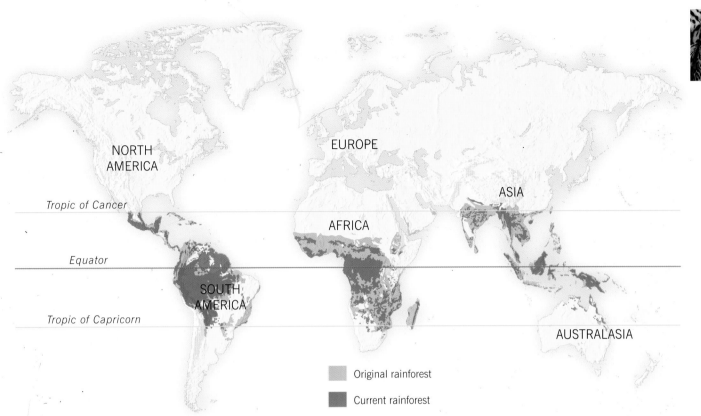

NORTH AMERICA

EUROPE

ASIA

Tropic of Cancer

AFRICA

Equator

SOUTH AMERICA

Tropic of Capricorn

AUSTRALASIA

Original rainforest

Current rainforest

Source: *World Conservation Monitoring Centre*

▲ *A map showing the extent of the world's tropical rainforests today, compared with their coverage 500 years ago, before large-scale deforestation began.*

▼ *Some mammals, such as this tapir, are often found in or near water. When frightened, tapirs plunge into the nearest water and swim away from harm.*

water if they sense danger. High above the forest floor, chattering monkeys swing and leap through the branches of rainforest trees, in search of edible fruits and seeds. In rivers and lakes, dolphins and giant otters surface for air as they search for fish. In the rainforests of Africa, chimpanzees move through the canopy, and rhinos, elephants and tigers roam the forest floor. Orang-utans and gibbons swing through the branches of rainforests in South-east Asia. In Australasia, unique species of rainforest kangaroos live in trees.

MAMMALS IN THE RAINFOREST

Mammals share their rainforest home with many species of birds, insects, amphibians and reptiles. Mammals are the most advanced group of animals on earth. All mammals are warm blooded and have a bony skeleton. Many have hair or fur on their bodies to keep them warm. Female mammals have special glands called mammary glands, which produce milk for feeding their young.

Tropical montane forest in Mexico. This type of forest is home to mammals that can adapt most easily to mountainous conditions.

LOWLAND RAINFOREST AND TROPICAL MONTANE FOREST

There are many different types of tropical rainforests. However, the types of rainforest that occur most widely are divided according to their height above sea level. These are lowland rainforest and tropical montane forest. Lowland rainforests, such as the Amazon rainforest, contain the majority of rainforest mammal species.

Tropical montane forest occurs on hills and mountains above 900 m, where conditions are generally cool. Montane forest trees are often hidden in dense mists, which has given rise to their alternative name, 'cloud forests'. Tropical montane forests are home to their own species of mammals, such as the spectacled bear and the water opossum, both of which live in mountainous regions of South America.

Spectacled bears are extremely rare and live only in tropical montane forests of South America.

THE JAGUAR

The jaguar is a cousin of the leopard. It lives in Central and South America, where its habitat extends from Mexico to Argentina. It is the largest carnivore in the Amazon rainforest, up to 2.5 m long, and weighing as much as 140 kg.

The jaguar usually lives in dense areas of rainforest and is an excellent climber. Its favourite food is the peccary, although it will also prey on deer and birds. The jaguar is a powerful swimmer, and also spends large amounts of time near water, waiting to catch fish and turtles. Jaguars also attack and eat caimans, which are a type of alligator.

There are fewer jaguars today than in the past. They are sometimes regarded as pests and killed in farming areas if they are a threat to livestock. They are also hunted illegally for their beautiful spotted skins.

▲ *Monkeys are important to the rainforest ecosystem because they help disperse the indigestible seeds of many rainforest plants.*

THE IMPORTANCE OF RAINFOREST MAMMALS

Mammals are a vital part of the rainforest food chain. Predators, such as jaguars and ocelots, for example, mainly feed on plant-eating mammals. This helps to control the numbers of animals that eat plants. Other mammals have lifestyles that benefit important plant species in the rainforest. Fruit-eating bats, for example, pollinate plants such as bananas and vanilla flowers. Some mammals are useful because they disperse seeds. Monkeys and tapirs, for example, often eat fruit and carry the indigestible seeds in their stomachs for many kilometres before expelling them from their bodies. The seeds germinate in a new part of the rainforest, so spreading the plant more widely.

2 THE DIVERSITY OF MAMMALS

THE RANGE OF MAMMALS

Around 65 million years ago, when the dinosaurs died out, mammals started to evolve. The mammals that were the strongest and adapted well to their environment survived, while others died out. Today, there are about 5,000 species of mammals. The world's rainforests are estimated to contain around half of all these species. The range of mammals in the rainforest extends from rainforest hippos weighing more than one tonne to minute tree shrews weighing just a few grammes.

After millions of years of evolution, many mammals have developed highly specialized lifestyles. While living far apart, some mammal species have evolved in rainforests in similar ways. For example, the pangolin of Africa and the tamandua of South America evolved on different continents, but are very similar animals. They are both about the same size and shape, they live in trees and eat only ants.

▲ The tree shrew is a tiny mammal. It is very similar to the first mammals that existed during the time of the dinosaurs.

◀ The pangolin is sometimes called a scaly anteater. Its diet is made up of ants and its body is covered with flat, bony scales.

OWL MONKEYS

Owl monkeys are a small species of monkey that live in the Amazon rainforest. On moonlit nights, owl monkeys search for fruits, seeds and flower nectar. It is unusual for monkeys to be nocturnal, and it is believed owl monkeys evolved these nocturnal habits because there is less competition for food at night than during the day.

The monkeys often make long, low calls like a hooting noise as they move around the trees. This helps male and female pairs of monkeys to locate each other or young to find their parents.

Owl monkeys usually rest during the daytime. They sleep in tree hollows, which are generally found amongst the vines and creepers that grow near rivers.

► *The tamandua is quite like the pangolin, but has tough hairs on its body rather than the bony scales found on the pangolin.*

Rainforest animals have adapted to their habitats. Some monkey species, for example, are able to use their tail like a fifth limb to help them move through the rainforest. Other species of monkey and sloth have developed special stomachs to enable them to eat poisonous leaves and fruit. Some squirrels have developed flaps of skin, which let them glide from one tree to another.

SECRETIVE LIVES

No one knows exactly how many rainforest species exist. Many rainforest mammals lead shy and secretive lives, and are rarely seen either by scientists or by local people. Even large mammals, such as the spectacled bear, are very rarely seen in their mountain habitat. Smaller mammals, such as the numerous species of opossums that inhabit the lowland rainforests of Central and South America, are not only very timid, but often only come out at night.

NUMBERS OF MAMMALS

Many of the mammals found in rainforests are small species, such as bats, rats, mice and porcupines. While rainforests appear to be rich in plants, little light reaches the deep forest floor so the vegetation at ground level is sparse. This means there is not very much food for the bigger animals to eat. Large mammals that live deep in the forest often have to travel long distances to find enough plant food. Because of this, fewer large mammals per hectare live in the rainforest than in other habitats, such as the savannah grasslands of Africa, which have rich and plentiful vegetation.

▲ Rainforests have a wide range of bats, including these flying foxes that live in the mangrove forests of Tanzania, in Africa.

RAINFOREST SECRETS

THE BIGGEST RODENT – THE CAPYBARA

The capybara lives in South America and is the world's biggest rodent. Capybaras are always found near water where they feed mainly on water plants. When frightened, they plunge into pools or rivers where they swim strongly, helped by their webbed feet. Above the water, just their nostrils, eyes and ears can be seen by predators. Capybaras are prey for jaguars, caimans and giant snakes called anacondas.

Capybaras are still fairly common in South America where they live in large groups. Their main threat is from humans. People hunt capybaras for their meat and skins and because they destroy their crops. In parts of the Amazon rainforest, especially near towns and cities, they have been over-hunted and have now almost completely disappeared.

▶ *Pygmy hippos are found in a very small area of the West African rainforest. Because of the lack of food in the rainforest, they are smaller than their relatives in other parts of the world.*

▼ *Many aquatic rainforest mammals are much larger than their relatives from other parts of the world. The world's largest species of otter is found in the Amazon rainforest.*

THE SIZE OF RAINFOREST SPECIES

The scarcity of food has affected the growth of the larger rainforest mammals. Many of the large mammals that live deep in the rainforest have evolved to become smaller than their relatives in other habitats. The pygmy hippo and the royal antelope from the rainforests of West Africa, and the Sumatran rhino from Indonesia, are smaller in size than their closest relatives in different habitats.

However, by contrast, rainforest mammals that live and feed in or near water can grow much larger than their relatives that live in other parts of the world. Rainforest plants are found in abundance along the banks of rivers and have provided plentiful food for mammals such as the capybara. Rivers are a good source of food for aquatic mammals. The giant otter is an example of a rainforest mammal that has evolved to be larger than its relatives because it has always inhabited rivers rich in fish.

ISOLATED SPECIES

Each rainforest has types of mammals that are unique to that area. Over millions of years, rainforests in different parts of the world have developed in isolation, as continents split apart. In Africa and South America, mammals such as monkeys started to evolve from a common ancestor before the continents were separated 100 million years ago. However, the continent of Australasia was isolated from the rest of the world millions of years before this common ancestor existed. In the rainforests of Australia and Papua New Guinea, other mammals evolved to take the place of these primates. Today, special types of tree kangaroos have similar positions in their rainforest ecosystem as monkeys have in other rainforests.

Many species of rainforest monkeys are unique to the continent where they live. Chimpanzees, for example, are only found in the rainforests of West and Central Africa. They developed after the South American continent separated from the African continent, so they are not found in South America. However, South America has about 77 species of primates, and half of these are only found in the Amazon rainforest. Some species of primates are even more localized. The golden lion tamarin, for example, is found in just a few thousand hectares of Atlantic forest on the coast of Brazil.

▲ Matchie's tree kangaroo lives in Papua New Guinea. It is an example of an animal that has evolved to live in the trees, much as monkeys do in other parts of the world.

RAINFOREST SECRETS

LEMURS – THE INDRI

The rainforest on the island of Madagascar is inhabited by many unusual species of mammals. Among these are the lemurs, which are often described as 'primitive monkeys'. Lemurs are descended from the same ancient ancestor as monkeys and apes. Over millions of years they have evolved into a large variety of species. The pygmy mouse lemur, for example, is so small that it could sit in an eggcup. The largest lemur, the indri (right) grows to over a metre long and weighs around 7 kg.

Humans first arrived in Madagascar, about 1,200 years ago. Lemurs were killed for food and parts of their habitat were gradually destroyed. Over hundreds of years, 15 species became extinct. There are now only about 50 species of lemur left.

The giant island of Madagascar, which lies to the south-east of Africa, split away from the African continent 150 million years ago. Monkeys did not evolve on this island in the same way as in other rainforests. Instead, different types of rainforest lemur evolved. Lemurs have long, slender bodies, long tails and thick, woolly fur. However, their lives are similar to monkeys found elsewhere.

◀ *Chimpanzees belong to a group of intelligent monkeys called apes. They evolved after the continents of Africa and South America had separated, and are only found in Africa.*

③ HOME AND HABITAT

DIFFERENT RAINFOREST HABITATS

Rainforests that are found in different parts of the world often look quite similar to each other, but each has unique conditions and different combinations of plant and animal species. The most widespread type of rainforest is lowland rainforest, such as the Amazon.

In the Amazon, the main division is between the *terra firme* (dry ground forest) and the *várzea* (flooded forest). In the *várzea*, parts of the rainforest are submerged for several months of each year, when the waters rise leaving only the tallest trees visible. Along coastal areas of lowland rainforests are mangrove forests, another important type of lowland rainforest.

On higher slopes are the tropical montane forests. Most mammals have adapted to particular types of forest, but some mammals can live in a variety of habitats. Pumas, for example, can thrive in most parts of both the tropical montane forest and lowland rainforest.

▲ *A typical interior of lowland rainforest near Belém in Brazil. The lowland areas of the Amazon rainforest are home to mammal species such as tapirs, jaguars and ocelots.*

SLOTHS – LIFE IN THE CANOPY

The sloth spends most of its life hanging upside down in a tree. Sloths are adapted to a sluggish pace of life, moving through the branches at a rate of one kilometre per hour, and eating leaves that most other mammals cannot digest. The sloth also has special hairs that have grooves to allow algae to grow in them. This helps to camouflage the sloth as it moves slowly through the vegetation of the canopy.

Although a sloth cannot walk well, it is perfectly adapted to hanging upside down, suspended on long, slender claws. It is so effortless for a sloth to hang upside down that when a sloth dies it remains hanging while it decomposes.

▲ Red colobus monkeys have specially adapted stomachs so they can eat leaves from the canopy.

▼ Giant anteaters are found on the floor of dry ground forest in the Amazon.

Fascinating Fact

The sloth has one of the smallest mammal brains – about the size of a small marble.

LEVELS OF LOWLAND RAINFOREST

Rainforest mammals are adapted to life at the different levels within a lowland rainforest. Some species of mammals, such as monkeys, sloths and bats spend most of their lives high up in the canopy. Others, such as various types of deer and anteaters, forage on the rainforest floor for plants or insects to eat. Tapirs, capybara, giant otters and jaguars spend much time searching for fish and other prey in rivers.

◀ Terra firme *forest in the Amazon rainforest is characterized by large trees which can grow to heights of over 70 m. Dry ground forest provides habitats for both ground and tree-living mammals.*

LOWLAND AMAZONIAN RAINFOREST

In the Amazon rainforest, most mammals live in the *terra firme* forest. Large herds of white-lipped peccaries, for example, can be found in this type of forest along with mammals such as anteaters and coatimundis. Many of the mammals that live in dry ground forest cannot get across rivers. Some species of marmoset, for example, are believed to have been isolated on 'islands' of dry land between rivers for tens of thousands of years.

The *terra firme* forests also have species of trees and other plants that are not found in other types of rainforest. Many species of mammals survive on very specific types of fruits, seeds and leaves that grow in the forest. Bats and monkeys often rely on the fruits and flower nectar from a limited number of tree species, and usually have to travel large distances between trees to find edible fruit, seeds or leaves.

▲ *The coatimundi is a type of raccoon that spends time both climbing among the trees and foraging for food on the ground of the Central and South American rainforests.*

FLOODED FOREST

Flooded areas occur in rainforests around the world, but the largest and most famous is the flooded forest in the upper Amazon near the city of Manaus, in Brazil. Here the water levels fall and rise by as much as 13 m between the dry and wet seasons. The types of trees that can survive this flooding are very different from those that are found in the dry ground forest. Many mammals that live in trees, such as sloths and squirrel monkeys, move out of the rainforest when it becomes flooded. Other species, such as the uakari monkey, have adapted to living in the flooded forest all year round and only come down to the ground in the dry season. Species such as dolphins and manatees can swim between the branches of the submerged trees in search of food during the flooded season.

▲ A typical view of the flooded forest of the upper Amazon as the waters begin to rise at the start of the flooded season.

RAINFOREST SECRETS

THE UAKARI MONKEY

The white uakari is found only in untouched areas of the flooded forest, east of the Amazon city of Manaus. It is a medium-sized monkey weighing between 2 and 4 kg. A white uakari is very distinctive, with a shaggy white coat, a short bushy tail and a spectacular red face.

Uakari monkeys spend most of their time in the canopy of the flooded forest. During the dry season they come down to ground level and search out seeds and fallen fruit. They have specially adapted teeth that allow them to open the husks of unripe fruits and seeds, and a special stomach to cope with the toxic chemicals used by plants to protect unripe seeds.

THE SPECTACLED BEAR

MANGROVE FOREST

Mangrove forest covers a much smaller area than *terra firme* forest – an area of about 2,400 sq km, which is similar to the size of the state of California, USA. Mangrove forests are frequently visited by mammals such as dolphins and manatees. Some types of vervet monkeys visit the coastal forest along the Indian Ocean coastline of Africa in search of crabs, shellfish, fruit and seeds. In other parts of the world, mammals such as the crab-eating raccoon also hunt and scavenge among the bell-shaped roots of mangrove trees.

The spectacled bear is South America's only species of bear. It lives mainly in tropical montane forest in the foothills of the Andes, although it occasionally visits lowland rainforests.

Spectacled bears eat mainly fruits, nuts, insects and leaves. One of their favourite foods are bromeliads (see above right). These plants grow on the branches of trees and the bears will climb up to eat the fleshy centres.

Each spectacled bear requires 6 sq km of undisturbed tropical montane forest for its survival. Spectacled bears are now very rare because large areas of tropical montane forest have been destroyed or disturbed.

◀ *Mangrove forests are not home to many species of mammals, although they are frequently visited.*

▲ Mountain gorillas are among the world's rarest mammals. They live in tropical montane forest in central African countries such as Rwanda, where they feed mainly on fruits and leaves.

TROPICAL MONTANE FOREST

There are many species of mammals that live in tropical montane forest. Montane forest trees are covered in many types of epiphytes, such as orchids and bromeliads. The plants that grow on the branches and trunks of these trees are a source of food for particular types of bats, opossums, spiny tree rats and spectacled bears. Because of the cooler temperatures that exist in montane forests, montane mammals often have thicker fur than the mammals that live in lowland rainforests. Tropical montane forest is home to the mountain gorilla, which is found only in very restricted areas of the forests in central Africa.

LIVING IN THE RAINFOREST

The lifestyle of mammals depends on the part of the rainforest they live in and the food they eat. Monkeys, for example, are well adapted to living in the canopy. They use their strong hands for gripping and their tail for balance to move quickly through the branches in search of fruit, nuts and leaves and can reach the emergent layers of the rainforest at a height of about 70 m above the canopy.

Other mammals are better adapted to living in the twilight world of the rainforest floor. Deer and tapirs feed on plants, armadillos search for insects among the vegetation and agoutis find nuts and seeds on the ground. Some mammals such as leopards roam the rainforest floor, but they are also excellent climbers and lie among the tree branches, silently waiting to ambush their prey. Aquatic mammals, such as dolphins and manatees, are well adapted to life in the water of lowland rainforests.

▲ Armadillos are common to the rainforests of South and Central America, where they feed mainly on a diet of insects.

▼ The Brazilian bare-faced tamarin thrives in the dense vegetation of rainforest, mainly along river banks.

RAINFOREST SECRETS

A MERMAID MYTH

The manatee (see right) is an aquatic mammal that is similar to a large seal. Manatees live in lowland rivers, and along mangrove coasts.

The Senegal manatees of West Africa are believed to have given rise to stories about mermaids. Mermaids were mythical creatures, half women and half fish. Sailors who saw manatees from a distance, cradling their young in their flippers, mistook them for mermaids breast-feeding their babies.

In the Amazon, manatees were once common, but they are now very rare. One species of manatee has already been hunted to extinction. In West Africa, fishermen set traps to catch manatees as they move into the mangrove swamps when the tide rises.

GROUPS OF MAMMALS

Mammals are often divided into groups that have similar lifestyles or distinctive features. For example, rodents such as rats, mice and squirrels form a distinct group because of their canine teeth. Aquatic mammals form another group. Animals that are carnivores, such as cats and raccoons, make up a group of meat-eaters, while herbivores, such as deer and elephants, make up a group of plant-eaters. Omnivores are a group that eat a variety of food. This includes primates, such as apes and monkeys. Bats make up a group of their own because they are the only mammals that can fly.

◀ *The green agouti is a rodent that feeds on nuts and seeds using its sharp teeth and strong jaw muscles to break open tough shells.*

◀ *The jaguar is the most fiercesome carnivore in the lowland forests of South and Central America. Like other carnivores it has large canine teeth to tear the flesh of its victim.*

Fascinating Fact

The jaguar spends a great deal of its time near water. It sometimes lures its prey by dangling its tail in the water and scooping up fish with its huge paws.

CATS

Six species of cat live in the rainforests of South and Central America. In the Amazon rainforest, cats are the main predators. They use their canine teeth for killing and tearing the flesh of prey. They also have sharp claws and powerful shoulders, and are capable of bringing down and killing large animals. Most types of cats, such as jaguars and margays, are solitary hunters and capture prey by moving stealthily through the rainforest undergrowth. The spots of cats such as the ocelot, margay and jaguar help to camouflage them in the dappled light of the rainforest floor.

THE PUMA

The puma is the most wide-ranging and successful cat species in the Americas. Pumas are able to thrive in any habitats where there are plenty of animals such as deer, agoutis and pacas, which are their prey.

Pumas are found throughout both lowland rainforest and tropical montane forest, but prefer dry ground where possible. They are equally well suited to many other types of environment, and can be found as far north as Canada and as far south as the tip of Chile.

RACCOONS AND WEASELS

The mammals that are part of the raccoon family live in Central and South America. These include the coatimundi, the crab-eating raccoon and the kinkajou, which is similar to the raccoon. Raccoons are mainly omnivores and eat insects, crabs, frogs and snakes as well as fruits and seeds. Members of the raccoon family are all good tree climbers and also feed on nesting birds.

There are eight species of mammal that make up the weasel family. They include skunks and otters. Members of the weasel family are very aggressive, and can kill and eat prey much larger than themselves.

Several species of otter live along the rivers of lowland rainforest in the Amazon and also thrive in the fast-flowing rivers and streams of tropical montane forest in South America.

▼ *The kinkajou is a type of raccoon that lives in the rainforests of South and Central America.*

ELEPHANTS

Some types of rainforest provide a home for a small number of large plant-eaters. In Africa, there are certain types of elephant that live only in the rainforest. They are a subspecies of the African elephant, and are generally much smaller than elephants that live in the savannah. Little is known about them because they lead secretive lives in some of the most inaccessible rainforest in the Congo basin. The Asian elephant, sometimes called the Indian elephant, is also a rainforest plant-eater, but few Asian elephants remain in the wild because they have been hunted and their habitat destroyed.

◀ *Asian elephants used to live in large numbers throughout the rainforests of Asia, but today there are only a few herds left. They usually feed on shoots, leaves and fruit.*

▼ *Congo rainforest cattle live in the world's second largest area of rainforest, which covers the Congo river basin in Africa.*

DEER AND CATTLE

Deer are also rainforest plant eaters. Deer originated in Asia and have only recently – about 12,000 years ago – crossed the Bering Strait into the Americas from Russia. Deer are common in Asia, where many species live, although in the South American rainforest only three species exist today.

Rainforest cattle do not exist in the wild in South or Central America and are found only in Africa and Asia. These mammals are typically smaller than domestic cattle. Today, large areas of rainforest land in the Amazon is used for herding domestic cattle.

RAINFOREST SECRETS

THE LOWLAND TAPIR

The largest plant-eater that lives on dry land in the Amazon rainforest is the lowland tapir, which can weigh up to 250 kg. It is an unusual animal, related to both the horse and the rhino, which have similar three-hoofed feet. Like horses and rhinos, tapirs have special stomachs where plant material is broken down into digestible materials. They have a short, prehensile upper lip that acts much like the trunk of an elephant, by reaching out and pulling leaves towards their mouth.

The lowland tapirs are mostly nocturnal and feed mainly on swamp plants, grass and fruits. They spend most of their time near waterside habitats although they can negotiate steep mountainsides and dry forest floors. When startled, they plunge into water and can swim quite long distances under the surface.

PECCARIES

Peccaries are mainly plant-eaters, despite their long, downward-pointing canine teeth. However, like most species of pig, they are omnivorous because they will eat insects and even small mammals on occasions. Their canine teeth are enlarged for defence and combat with other peccaries.

▲ Collared peccaries live in small family groups of about six to nine individuals.

White-lipped peccaries move in large herds of 50–300 individuals, for safety against predators. Collared peccaries, by contrast, live fairly solitary lives in small family groups. To avoid being heard by predators, small groups of collared peccaries move silently through the rainforest.

Fascinating Fact
Peccaries have such poor eyesight that they will walk right up to a person who is standing still.

Large primates, such as chimpanzees and gorillas, are found in Africa, while orang-utans and gibbons live in South-east Asia. Because the rainforests of the Americas do not contain any large apes, large monkeys have evolved to fill similar positions to apes in their ecosystems.

LARGE MONKEYS

Large monkeys include spider, woolly and howler monkeys, all of which weigh more than 4 kg when fully grown. They mainly eat fruits and leaves. Large monkeys reproduce very slowly. Female woolly monkeys, for example, first give birth when they are between six and eight years old, and then produce just one baby every other year.

MEDIUM-SIZED MONKEYS

Medium-sized monkeys, including the sakis, uakaris and capuchin monkeys, are found in the Amazon, and weigh between 2 and 4 kg. They have large lower canine teeth that are used to split open the husks of unripe fruit and nuts. Capuchin monkeys often forage in groups of five to twenty monkeys, eating seeds, fruits, insects, eggs, lizards and even small mammals, such as opossums.

▲ Orang-utans are the second largest apes in the world. They are superb tree climbers at all levels of the rainforest.

◄ The brown capuchin monkey eats a more varied diet than many other species of monkey.

Fascinating Fact

Colobus monkeys have special stomachs that allow them to eat fruits and seeds which are deadly poisonous to other animals.

RAINFOREST SECRETS

PREHENSILE TAILS

Some species of monkey in South and Central America have developed a prehensile tail, which is a tail that they can use as a 'fifth limb'. Woolly monkeys (see right) and spider monkeys can use their tails for extra balance or to hang upside down, allowing them to use both hands and feet while feeding. It also allows these monkeys to spread their weight better on the branches, and find food that would otherwise be out of reach.

In the Amazon rainforest, several other types of mammals have developed prehensile tails, including the tree tamandua (also known as the tree anteater), the carnivorous kinkajou and several species of opossum.

▼ A pygmy marmoset holding the tail of a partly eaten lizard.

SMALL MONKEYS

In the Amazon rainforest, there are numerous small monkeys. The smallest primates are the marmosets and tamarins, including the pygmy marmoset which weighs just 100 g. Marmosets and tamarins both have special, sharp canine teeth for gouging holes in tree trunks, and feed extensively on plant sap. Small monkeys include the squirrel and titi monkeys, which are very agile and scamper along the branches searching for seeds, fruits, insects and leaves. Squirrel monkeys live in large groups in the middle levels of the rainforest. They often have their homes near rivers, where there are plenty of branches and vines.

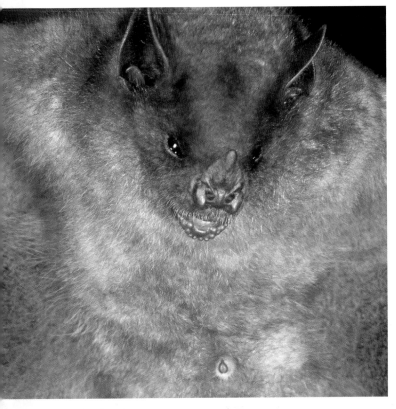

▲ Many bats, such as this one from the tropical montane forest in Ecuador, eat only fruit.

BATS

Bats are the only mammals that can fly. They are the second largest group of mammals, after rodents, with 950 species worldwide. In the rainforests of Central America, for example, there are more bat species than all other mammal species combined.

Bats are able to fly because their arms and fingers are covered in a remarkable thin, rubbery skin to form wings. In the rainforests of South America, all the species of bats use sound to help them fly at night, and to locate food. The bats make a high clicking sound, which humans cannot hear.

VAMPIRE BATS

There are three species of vampire bats in the rainforests of South and Central America. These bats feed on the blood of birds and mammals, including the blood of humans on occasions. They hunt at night, and attack their victims as they sleep. Vampire bats use their razor-sharp teeth to make a quick and painless wound. They do not suck blood from the body but lick it up with their tongues as it flows from the wound. Vampire bats have a special substance in their saliva that stops the blood from clotting until the bat has finished feeding.

▼ The shape of the parkia flower, found in West Africa, makes it easy for bats to feed from it and so pollinate the plant.

▲ A Geoffroy's long-nosed bat from the rainforests of French Guiana in South America, feeding on nectar and taking pollen from a rainforest flower. Many species of bats pollinate rainforest plants.

Listening to the echoes of these sounds, they can judge where objects are, and follow the path of insects in total darkness. This is called echo-location.

Bats are extremely well adapted to life in the rainforest. During the day, they normally sleep together in big groups, hanging upside down with their wings folded. At night they wake up to feed. Bats usually eat fruit and the nectar from flowers or insects. As they feed on the nectar, the tip of the tongue takes up pollen along with the nectar and pollinates the flower. Bats are also important in spreading seeds. When they eat fruit, such as figs, the seeds get passed through their bodies and are deposited as waste. In this way, the seeds are spread throughout the rainforest.

5 DISAPPEARING MAMMALS

WHY ARE MAMMALS DISAPPEARING?

The numbers of many rainforest mammal species have declined rapidly over the last thirty years. Mammals such as mountain gorillas, spectacled bears, tigers, rhinos, manatees and orang-utans have declined so drastically that they are in danger of becoming extinct. The number of golden lion tamarins in Brazil's Atlantic forest, for example, fell to a few hundred individuals in the 1990s, and there are now less than 800 mountain gorillas left in Africa.

There are many reasons why some rainforest mammals are disappearing. However, the largest single cause for their decline is the destruction of their rainforest habitat.

A large rainforest tree is felled in the rainforest of Cameroon in West Africa. Logging in West Africa is causing the destruction of the habitats of many rainforest mammals.

Fascinating Fact

A giant sloth that stood 4 m tall and weighed about a tonne, became extinct in the Amazon about 10,000 years ago.

Millions of people in Africa eat 'bush meat'. Bush meat can be any sort of meat from wild mammals, and includes meat from monkeys, deer, manatees and large rodents.

LINKS

Medicines and Charms

The organs of particular rainforest mammals are believed by many people to have special magical or medicinal properties. In India and a number of other Asian countries, for example, the gall bladder of a sloth bear is reputed to cure liver and stomach problems. Thousands of these wild animals are killed in order to use their organs for such purposes.

In the Amazon and Andes mountains, parts of jaguars and spectacled bears are sold as medicines or as charms.

▼ Small monkeys such as this squirrel monkey are popular as pets and many are taken from the wild to supply the pet trade.

Large carnivores are also shot because of the risk that they will kill someone or eat livestock. They are hunted for food, for their skins and for their internal organs, which are believed to have medicinal properties.

THE PET TRADE

Tens of thousands of rainforest mammals, such as small monkeys, are trapped and sold as pets. It is also common for the parents of mammals such as orang-utans to be killed so their young can be sold to people who live in nearby towns or cities. Sometimes they are sold abroad. In the Amazon region, monkeys such as squirrel monkeys and capuchins are regularly kept as house pets. In the Indian sub-continent, some species of bear are captured and made to dance to earn money for their owners.

◀ A jaguar being skinned in an Amazonian village. The meat will be eaten and the skin sold.

▼ A young boy with a monkey which has been killed for food in Cameroon.

HUNTING

Rainforest mammals have been hunted for more than a million years to provide food for people to eat. The very first people to move into the rainforest are believed to have been hunters. Until recently, the number of people living in the rainforests was very low. Today, there are more than 150 million people living in, or close to, the rainforests and hunting is having a serious effect on mammals. Animals are not only hunted for food; many rare animals are also killed by professional hunters for sport. In parts of Africa, there is a large trade in bush meat from animals such as deer and monkeys. In the Amazon, as elsewhere, manatees are hunted for their meat. One species of manatee has already become extinct, and the three remaining species are endangered.

SKIN TRADE

The hunting of animals for their skins is another human activity that is causing mammal numbers to decline in rainforests. Tigers, jaguars and ocelots have been hunted heavily because their beautiful skins can be sold for large sums of money. The killing continues, even though it is often illegal. For poor people in the rainforest, selling skins is one way to earn money to feed their families. On a bigger scale, criminal organizations often smuggle skins to wealthy buyers in the rich countries of the world.

▼ *A peccary skin is dried on a frame before being sold in a local Amazonian town.*

RAINFOREST SECRETS

HUNTING THE GIANT OTTER

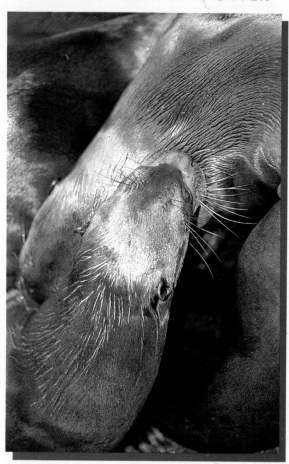

In the Amazon, the giant otter has suffered at the hands of people. Otters have been heavily hunted for their skins, and killed because they compete with people for fish in rivers. One of the reasons why giant otters have suffered so badly is that they are easily accessible to hunters. Otters live on river banks where they cannot easily hide. The sound of giant otters noisily squeaking and surfacing with loud snorts, makes them easy targets for hunters.

DISAPPEARING HABITATS

The most serious threat to rainforest mammals is the loss of their rainforest homes. When rainforests are cut down or burned, it can take hundreds of years for them to recover. Without the rainforest insects and plants that they need to survive, many mammals are forced to move away, or risk dying of hunger.

As rainforests are destroyed, mammals are forced to live in smaller and smaller areas of rainforest. Some types of rainforests have been so seriously affected that they are in danger of disappearing entirely, along with the animals that live in them. The Atlantic forest in Brazil, for example, has been reduced to just 5 per cent of its original area, and the same is true of the rainforests of Madagascar, which are considered to be the most threatened rainforests in the world.

◄ Drilling for oil and the construction of long pipelines across the Amazon rainforest is having a major impact on mammal populations.

Fascinating Fact

There are now believed to be less than 400 Sumatran rhinos left in the wild.

HUMAN ACTIVITIES

Human activities play a large part in rainforest destruction. Huge areas are being cut down to produce timber, firewood, charcoal and wood pulp for paper. Vast areas are being cut down and converted into agricultural land.

LINKS

Burning the Rainforest

Throughout the world, burning is destroying huge areas of rainforest. In agricultural areas in Madagascar, for example, burning is used to clear land after the rice harvest. If the fires get out of control they spread to the national parks (see left) where lemurs are threatened. After the fires die away, rats move into the areas and prevent the land from recovering quickly. In the Amazon, burning destroys thousands of square kilometres of rainforest each year. The fires are so regular that it is called the burning season. This is a threat to animals that find it difficult to escape such as sloths, primates, armadillo and young deer.

Soya bean production in the Amazon and oil palm plantations in Africa and Asia have caused the loss of millions of square kilometres of rainforest. Building dams, digging mines and the expansion of towns and cities have also led to rainforest loss.

▶ Thousands of square kilometres of rainforest in the Amazon have been destroyed to make way for cattle ranching. This area of rainforest is in Acre State, Brazil.

35

⑥ CONSERVATION

◀ *Many environmental organizations are campaigning to save the remaining habitat of the orang-utan, and supporting projects that are aimed at protecting them.*

▼ *Tigers are now very rare. There are believed to be only a few thousand tigers left in India in the wild. To help protect them, it has become illegal to hunt tigers or sell their skins.*

SAVING THE SPECIES

The numbers of rare mammals such as tigers, orang-utans and manatees are so low that urgent action is needed if they are to survive even the next 20 years. Fortunately, there are many excellent campaigning organizations highlighting their plight and working hard to conserve species of rainforest mammals. Many rainforest communities have their own rules and ways of living that help ensure the survival of rare species.

The successful protection and conservation of rare rainforest mammal species is not easy, but there are a variety of ways in which people are trying to help. Organizations such as WWF and Friends of the Earth (FOE) campaign for the protection of rainforests, and for a better balance between the needs of wildlife, rainforest people and businesses who wish to develop the rainforests.

LINKS

Research in Madagascar

In Madagascar, around 95 per cent of the rainforest has been destroyed. Scientists are now carrying out research into how quickly certain types of mammals can return to a rainforest area, after it has been burned. The researchers hope to understand which animals can adapt to a renewed forest most easily. They also want to discover if there are ways of speeding up the regeneration of the rainforests to help the mammals.

In order to undertake research, scientists have to set traps to catch rainforest mammals. They are caught by pit traps (see far right) where a plastic barrier guides the mammals towards a container where they are caught and collected. The animals are weighed and measured (see right) before being released with an identification tag.

RESEARCH

The role of researchers in conservation is an important one. Scientists carry out research to estimate the numbers of rare animals, and to study how particular mammals live. Some rare species rely on certain types of food and special habitats. The spectacled bear, for example, needs to reach the bromeliads that grow on the branches of trees. Scientist have found out that the bears cannot live in areas that have been replanted recently, because the young trees are too weak for a bear to climb up and reach their food.

PROTECTED AREAS

One of the ways of helping rare rainforest mammals to survive is by protecting the rainforests in which they live. If the areas are large enough, even large mammals such as rhinos, tigers and elephants can be given a good chance of survival. WWF and other organizations have successfully campaigned for protected areas to be set up all over the world. These can take the form of national parks, nature reserves, community managed land, forest reserves, and rainforest corridors linking larger areas of rainforest.

There have been many campaigns for the protection of some of the most popular rainforest species. As a result, there are special parks for animals such as jaguars, lemurs and rainforest rhinos. Many campaigns focus on the best-known and most 'appealing' species as a means of getting an area protected. This also helps less 'appealing' mammals, such as rainforest bats or anteaters, which also benefit whenever an area of rainforest becomes protected.

▲ Indigenous people play an important part in conservation. This area of tropical montane forest in southern Mexico is owned, managed and protected by local Zapotec people.

▼ The Cockscomb Wildlife Sanctuary, in Belize in Central America, was established for the protection of jaguars in 1984.

▲ Udzungwa Mountain Forest in Tanzania is a national park that provides a home to some of Africa's rarest species of monkey.

INTERNATIONAL LAW

Over the last few decades, wildlife has been given much more protection by the introduction of new national and international laws. In many countries, there are national laws that aim to stop the hunting of rare mammals. International laws prevent skins, ivory and other animal products from rare animals being traded around the world. Under the United Nation's Convention on Biological Diversity, countries agree to help protect rare species from becoming extinct.

LINKS

Laws against International Trade

The Convention in the Trade of Endangered Species of flora and fauna (CITES) is an international law preventing the international trade in rare species of plants and animals.

This law has been effective in reducing the trade in rare animal skins, such as these ocelot skins (see right). There used to be a major trade in skins of rare mammals, such as tigers, jaguars and giant otters.

Today, some attempts are made to smuggle in skins from these mammals, but customs officers at major international airports search passengers and cargo for illegal animal products.

A squirrel monkey is one of the small monkeys that benefits from disturbances in the rainforest caused by small-scale agriculture.

▼ Rainforest that is recolonized after being deforested provides ideal conditions for the emperor tamarin. It likes to climb on the trunks of the new, small trees that grow close to one another.

SHARING THE RAINFOREST

For the descendants of people who have lived in the rainforest for thousands of years, sharing the rainforest with the animals is a natural way of life. However, there are people who have migrated to the rainforest because they have nowhere else to live. Some of these people may use the rainforest in a wasteful or destructive way. Destroying the rainforest on a local scale can affect both communities and wildlife. Organizations such as WWF recognize that people have to make a living in the rainforests so they support projects and communities that use the rainforest in a sustainable way that benefits both the people and the animals. Small-scale agriculture can help the rainforest. In Brazil, it was discovered that small primates, such as marmosets, thrive where people cut down small patches of rainforest. The young trees that recolonize these cut areas provide a suitable habitat and an important source of food for these small primates.

DOLPHINS

In the rivers and lakes of the Amazon rainforest there are two types of dolphin – the pink river dolphin and the grey dolphin. Pink river dolphins (see right) eat between 4 and 5 kg of fish a day, and are often in direct competition with local fishermen. Despite this competition, indigenous rainforest people do not usually hunt these mammals. This is mainly due to the myths and stories that surround dolphins. In some areas of the Amazon, people believe that dolphins can walk on land at night, as humans. In other areas, dolphins are linked to the powerful spirit of the moon.

▼ *Small primates can thrive in areas where the rainforest has been cut down and recolonized.*

MAINTAINING POPULATIONS

In traditional rainforest communities, there are often rules that help maintain rainforest mammal populations. In the Amazon, for example, indigenous hunters will not kill an animal if it is with its young. They also have rules about how many animals can be killed.

Traditional beliefs have also helped to maintain mammal populations. In the Andes, for example, many indigenous communities do not hunt spectacled bears because they believe these bears communicate with the gods who live in the dense clouds at the top of the mountains. In the Amazon, many indigenous groups have beliefs about dolphins, which has saved these mammals from being hunted.

ZOOS AND CONSERVATION

Zoos are important centres for studying the behaviour of animals as it is much easier to learn about them in captivity. Zoos and other scientific research centres also have an important role in the conservation of rainforest mammals. Some wild animals such as the buffy-headed capuchin monkeys from Brazil, and the mountain gorillas of Rwanda, are so rare that without help, they will become extinct. Modern zoos not only have some rainforest animals for the public to see but are also trying to increase their numbers in the wild. To do this, the animals are bred in captivity.

▲ Children learning about a conservation project from a display at Chester Zoo, England.

LINKS

Conservation in Action

Like many major zoos worldwide, Chester Zoo, in north-west England, runs a number of conservation projects aimed at increasing the understanding of animals in the wild.

Since 1996, Chester Zoo has also been helping to breed the rare buffy-headed capuchin monkey from the Atlantic forest (see below). It has also successfully bred orang-utans.

In 2000, Chester Zoo signed an agreement with Chengdu Zoo in China to collaborate on research into the endangered panda.

▶ *A scientist in the Atlantic rainforest of Brazil uses tracking equipment to locate a young golden lion tamarin that has a radio collar fitted. This enables scientists to follow and study groups of tamarins in dense rainforest.*

Fascinating Fact

Since 1972, a campaign run by WWF called Project Tiger has led to the setting up of 23 special tiger reserves to help conserve tigers.

The young are released into protected areas to increase the wild populations. Often the zookeepers have to teach the young animals how to live and survive away from captivity. Scientists may use tracking devices in order to locate and follow the animals they have released in the wild.

SUPPORTING ENVIRONMENTAL ORGANIZATIONS

Campaigns are run by organizations such as WWF to highlight the plight of animals such as tigers, gorillas and jaguars. These organizations also fund conservation activities around the world and champion laws to stop the trade in rare animal products. Joining and supporting environmental organizations is one way that people who live a long way away from rainforests can help to protect and conserve rainforest mammals.

The Amazon rainforest is currently undergoing large-scale logging, and the clearance of land for ranching and agriculture. The rate of destruction in the Amazon is showing no signs of slowing down. The world's growing population puts great demands on rainforest resources. Rainforests often exist in the world's poorest countries, and their governments often have little option but to exploit their resources to earn the money needed for development and repaying the debts they may owe to richer countries.

Rainforests such as the Amazon need sustainable development, which meets the needs of local people as well as conservation. There are economic activities that can be undertaken in rainforests that can provide people with a living and protect the rainforests.

▲ An area of flooded forest in the Amazon that is protected for the future. This will benefit species of monkey such as the uakari, and aquatic mammals such as dolphins, manatees and otters.

DEVELOPING ECOTOURISM

Many tourists are willing to take holidays to see rare mammals in rainforest areas. Encouraging ecotourism is a positive step to take in rainforest countries. Ecotourism is a growing industry that preserves the rainforest habitats and the species that live in them. It is also a way of providing income for local people in rainforest areas. They can earn more money through tourism than through activities such as hunting mammals, selling skins, deforestation and growing crops.

▼ Ecotourism is being encouraged as a way of helping the rainforests. This walkway in a tourist area near Manaus helps people to locate the animals.

RAINFOREST SECRETS

GOLDEN LION TAMARIN

In early 2001 a landmark event took place in a small part of Brazil's Atlantic forest. The numbers of one of the world's rarest primates, the golden lion tamarin had exceeded 1,000 individuals for the first time in many years. Zoos from all over the world and environmental organizations such as WWF had been working for 20 years to try and stop this small primate from becoming extinct. Young animals bred in zoos were released into the wild and nesting boxes for the tamarins were provided. Local farmers made parts of their land into sanctuaries for the tamarins. Eventually, the decline in numbers was halted.

This success proves that if we take action, we can save many of the world's endangered species from becoming extinct.

▼ *Several new species of woolly monkey similar to this were found in the Amazon rainforest in 2000.*

THE FUTURE

The future of many rainforest mammals is uncertain. With the current rate of rainforest destruction, there is a real possibility that in the future many rare species may exist only in parks and zoos. It is only by protecting rainforests and undertaking conservation programmes that the future for mammals can look very much brighter. It is up to all of us to ensure that all rainforest wildlife can be guaranteed a better future.

Fascinating Fact

At least eight new species of monkey have been discovered in the Amazon rainforest since 1999.

GLOSSARY

Orang-utan.

ape A large monkey-like mammal such as a gorilla, chimpanzee, orang-utan or gibbon. Unlike a monkey, an ape has no tail.

aquatic An animal or plant that lives in or near water.

bromeliads A group of plants that come from the Americas and have a rosette of spiny leaves.

camouflaged Having colours, shapes or patterns that help an animal blend in with its surroundings.

canine A large tooth near the front of the mouth.

canopy The layer of trees between the rainforest floor and the tallest towering treetops.

captivity Being kept in a particular area, held in by a cage or fence.

conservation Looking after the environment and its resources.

ecosystem A community of different species and the environment they live in.

ecotourism Activities where tourists visit natural environments with an interest in conserving them.

emergents Tall trees that tower above the canopy, often with a cauliflower-shaped crown.

endangered When a species is at risk of dying out.

epiphytes Plants that grow on other plants.

evolve When a species of any living organism develops naturally over many generations.

extinct When a species of any living organism, such as an animal or plant no longer exists.

food chain A series of organisms in a habitat. Each one is dependent on the next for food.

habitat The natural home of a particular plant or animal.

mammary glands Special organs that are unique to female mammals and produce milk for their young.

mangroves A swamp forest found on tropical and sub-tropical tidal mud flats.

national parks Parks which are recognized by national governments as important areas for conservation.

nature reserves Areas of land that are set up for the protection of wildlife.

pollinate To transfer pollen from the male to the female parts of a flower.

predators Animals that naturally prey on other animals.

prehensile Part of an animal's body that can grab or act like a limb.

prey An animal that is hunted and killed by another for food.

primates Highly evolved species of mammals that include lemurs, monkeys, apes and humans.

sap The vital liquid that circulates inside plants.

savannah Open grasslands in tropical or subtropical areas. Few bushes or trees grow in these habitats.

species A group of animals or plants that are similar to one another and can breed together.

FURTHER INFORMATION

BOOKS TO READ
Antonio's Rainforest by Anna Lewington (Hodder Wayland, 1998)

Closer Look at the Rainforest by Selina Wood (Franklin Watts, 1996)

Journey into the Rainforest by Tim Knight (Oxford University Press, 2001)

Jungle by Theresa Greenaway (Dorling Kindersley, 1994)

Rainforest Animals (Two-Can, 1999)

Secrets of the Rainforest by Michael Chinery (Cherrytree, 2001)

The Wayland Atlas of Rainforests by Anna Lewington (Hodder Wayland, 1996)

WEBSITES
There are many websites about the rainforests. Type in key words to search for the information you need, or visit the following sites:

Passport to the Rainforest
http://www.passporttoknowledge.com/rainforest/
Includes map, graphics, images and information about plants and animals.

Rainforest Action Network
http://www.ran.org/
Facts about rainforest people and animals. Includes action that can be taken to conserve the rainforests.

Rainforest Conservation Fund
http://www.conservation.org/
Provides species data for plants and animals. There is also news, projects and articles.

Rainforest Information Centre
http://www.rainforestinfo.org.au
News, information, ecology and conservation. Includes a links page for children.

Species Survival Network CITES Conference
http://www.defenders.org/cites
Information on CITES conferences, which discuss the world's endangered species. It includes appendixes of endangered animals and plants.

World Rainforest Movement
http://www.wrm.org.uy/
Includes information on rainforests by country and by subject.

WWF–UK
http://www.wwf-uk.org/
In addition to its main website in the UK, the environmental organization has a number of sites devoted to different campaigns.
http://www.panda.org/
The international site for WWF.
http://www.panda.org/forest4life
The forests for life campaign.

Visit learn.co.uk for more resources.

CD ROM
Rainforest (Interfact) by Lucy Baker and Jason Page (Two-Can, 1998)

VIDEO
The Decade of Destruction by Adrian Cowell (Central Independent Television, 1991)

ADDRESSES OF ORGANIZATIONS
Friends of the Earth, 26-28 Underwood Street, London N1 7JQ Tel: 020 7490 1555
http://www.foe.co.uk/
Greenpeace, Canonbury Villas, London N1 2PN Tel: 020 7865 8100
http://www.greenpeace.org.uk/
Oxfam, Oxfam House, Banbury Road, Oxford, OX2 7DZ Tel: 01865 312610
http://www.oxfam.org.uk/
Survival International, 6 Charterhouse Buildings, London EC1M 7ET Tel: 020 7687 8700
http://www.survival-international.org/
WWF–UK, Panda House, Weyside Park, Godalming, Surrey GU7 1XR Tel: 01483 426444
http://www.wwf-uk.org/

INDEX

Picture acknowledgements:
All photographs are by Edward Parker with the exception of the following: OSF 41 top (Konrad Wothe); Still Pictures 8 (Roland Seitre) 9 (Jany Sauvenet), 12 (Klein/Hubert), 13 top (Dominique Halleux), 15 (Roland Seitre), 19 (T. Geer), 20 top & 23 bottom (Norbert Wu), 25 right (Roland Seitre), 26 top (J.J Alcalay), 28 bottom (Gunter Zeisler), 29 top (Daniel Heuclin); WWF-UK 13 & 36 bottom (David Lawson). Artwork is by Peter Bull.